CASSANDRA

by Rose Goodbody

Content warning
This play contains brief mention of multiple distressing topics, including but not limited to sexual assault, self-harm, suicide, discrimination/bigotry and death.

Copyright © 2018 by Rose Goodbody

All rights reserved. No part of this play may be reproduced in any manner whatsoever without written permission except in the case of brief quotations embodied in critical articles and reviews.

First printing, 2025

I wrote this play for me.

I want to thank:

Ollie, who believed in it.
Séamus for loving what was broken.
&
Lyna, for performing it so beautifully.

Rebecca, I wouldn't have written this
if I hadn't known you.

PREFACE

Cassandra was first written for Found In Translation Theatre, with director and dramaturge Ollie Harrington, and performed in June 2018. A subversive adaptation of Aeschylus' 'Agamemnon', it debuted at the Blue Elephant Theatre. Two years later, Ollie & I held two R&D weekends to rework the play thanks to a grant from the Hellenic Society, which promotes engagement with Greek culture across the ages.

Now adapted for the page, this play has always been half prose, half poem. I've taken liberties in this version that I wouldn't have for a play text, and I encourage interpretations.

It's long been a trope that those who go into the arts are all tortured souls, using their pain to create beauty. While this might be true, it's only because everyone is a tortured soul in their own way. It is a truth of humanity.

I studied Aeschylus' *Agamemnon* in school, and I often credit Cassandra's small role as the only reason I could pay attention in class. Years later, a fierce desire to explore more of her character, and my own past, drove me to start adapting the play around Cassandra. I felt connected to her story.

During my early writing process, I was directly lifting lines for Cassandra from my own diaries, notes, and poems. The personal nature of the words made it hard to share drafts with other creatives for feedback, both the positive and the negative. So, while the show's first performance at the Blue Elephant Theatre was one of my proudest and most healing moments, the play wasn't the best it could be. And after that, I knew it.

In many ways *Cassandra* was too ambitious a play for us as emerging creatives in 2018 and even in 2020, those few months before the pandemic. It had its own music composed for it, its own choreography, a cast of six people and three creatives meaning we would have struggled to afford taking it on tour. But everyone that worked on it was so kind, and so supportive, and believed in sharing it.

So where do you turn when your script has gone stagnant? I couldn't work on it any further without fresh insight, without opening it up to others and hearing some genuine feedback. For me it meant taking plunge, but it also meant gathering a room full of trusted creatives for their insight and wisdom. With a generous grant from the Hellenic Society, we were able to run two weekends of R&D workshops with the FIT Theatre family.

It was incredible to hand my script over to this talented group who each had their own understanding of my words. Before we started, I thought I had said all I could about the issues facing abused and voiceless women. But after the first day of workshopping, I stayed up until four A.M. writing a new scene to try out the next morning. There may have been some teething moments where I had to sit on my hands and bite my tongue, but suddenly the gaps in my script felt fillable and we found new life in the story.

We took a few months break (it was Christmas and we all had presents to buy, family to see) but by the next R&D in March I had drafted three fresh scenes and made tweaks to clarify some of the play's most crucial speeches. In the months following our first run of *Cassandra,* I had really struggled to find the strength to reconnect with my characters, but now I was exploring them with a team that made it much easier for me to reexamine the work and do justice to its concepts.

Cassandra is still my favourite play, and I think that's allowed. Even working on editing it for print release has reminded me how much room there is for this to continue growing, and I hope it will be on the stage again in the future.

But for now, I'm just so proud of how it has matured, and so grateful to all that helped me get here. It gives me the impetus to tackle other ancient stories that I could lend that voice to. I'm definitely not done yet.

CHARACTERS

CASSANDRA
Priestess of Apollo and princess of Troy

APOLLO
God of the sun and prophecy

CLYTEMNESTRA
Queen of Mycenae, mother of Iphigenia, Helen of Troy's sister

AGAMEMNON
King of Mycenae, commander of the Achaeans during the Trojan War

THE WATCHER
Tasked with watching for AGAMEMNON'S return from Troy

THE ADVISOR
Advisor to the King, left behind to monitor CLYTEMNESTRA

CASSANDRA

CASSANDRA is alone.

She could be anywhere,
any time,
and nowhere,
always.

CASSANDRA: The trouble with trying to express experiences like this… is that it's so obvious to the person talking that we just can't communicate. The very act of telling the story robs us of the emotion; I can't tell you what happened *and* show you how it made me feel.

If I break down, if I rock on the spot, if I scream and cry and give you outward demonstrations of inner turmoil, you'll shush me. Or comfort me, tell me it's okay and I don't have to explain, because what could explain this? If you can get me to stop crying, I'll feel better, problem solved.

Let me tell you, all that is very therapeutic for me, in the moment. The problem comes later when I'm staring at a door, gripped in a panic, and you're staring at me, thinking... Why is a house freaking you out?

Well, I've never been able to explain before.

She rallies her courage to go on, her pain not enough to stop her now.

It comes in a rush.
Desperate to get it out, she needs to be heard,
needs someone to listen to her.

CASSANDRA: We met in the summer, when the sun was warm, and soulful, full of promises that everything would always be as it was then. There would always be olives and wine, I would forever be young, carefree, beautiful.

And he fed me compliments like sweet grapes, with perfect outer shells that later would burst within me and cause joy afresh. I'd be reminded of him and my cheeks would blush to think of how he saw me.

Divinity incarnate,
ethereal APOLLO's voice joins her,

*surrounds her,
encroaching and consuming.*

*APOLLO is there and not there,
a memory,
an ever present entity.*

APOLLO: You make me crazy.
        You make me break all the rules.
        I would do anything to make you happy.

*CASSANDRA leans into that voice.
She's missing it; feeling protective of this memory,*

*of when these words were said to her,
of when she believed them,
when she loved the person saying them.*

*It's wistful, this bittersweet feeling.
Grief.*

CASSANDRA: But you catch more flies with honey than with vinegar. His promises that he cared about me, that he wanted me to be happy? They were as true as the promises of that very same sun in the summer when the skies are clear.

Then clouds roll in, and on, and over me until water vapour is all I can breathe, and I'm drowning all over again.

He's all consuming and he knew it.

Those promises become demands, with:

APOLLO: You said you loved me,

CASSANDRA: And…

APOLLO: If you cared about me you'd accept my gift.

She flinches.
She sighs.
She goes on…
She must.

CASSANDRA: This, oh so generous gift that I never wanted or asked for, this thing that terrifies me and fills me with dread. I predict that prediction will make me miserable; I know I need to say no.

APOLLO: I want you to have it, it's a gift, why can't you just be grateful?

CASSANDRA: My heart breaks to see him sad, and to know the cause of that sadness lies with me. So I buckle. I'm the terrible one for not being grateful, when he's offering me something many beg him for.

Things don't get better. I can't see that they're getting worse.

We leave CASSANDRA
and come to a cliffside.
Not too far from the great kingdom, Mycenae.

Before us, leagues of a cursed sea,
small islands, rolling hills.

Here, an old woman looks out over the distance.
Unceasingly.

She's tired, weary,

but still she stares.

WATCHER: Ten years! Ten long years! I've been watching and waiting and waiting and watching. What's in the rota for little ol' me today? Will it be some watching, or waiting? Surprise! It's both.

I'm like a pining puppy just sat as high as I can get, waiting until my master comes home and throws me a bone. And still nothing changes. Well, the stars change with the seasons, but then the seasons repeat and with them the stars. After ten years, watching stars, I feel like I know them as friends.

I had to make sure I knew each one, you see, so I wouldn't mistake a star for this beacon light I'm supposed to wait for…

And if it ever does light up in the distance it'll be full of the vengeful fire of men and gods wanting to make other people suffer. Fire from burning Troy to the ground, just to drag back Helen because some King thinks she's his.

Well, I don't want it. I hope that fire never spreads here from Troy.

With every passing moment without our
master's return, we see the women of Mycenae
stepping up to take the slack that the young
men left behind when they went to fight other
young men. And now we're left with the old,
preying on those same young women who carry
the weight of a nation.

The ADVISOR,
a middling man,
arrives in time to scoff.

Smarmy, know-it-all, a true politician.

He disapproves of anything
CLYTEMNESTRA does.
As though it were his hobby.

ADVISOR: With all your moaning you are right about one
thing: the city is certainly suffering at the hands
of these women. Mycenae desperately needs its
brave men back.

WATCHER: Well what do you mean by that?

ADVISOR: As much as our Queen wishes she were a man, and as much as she pretends to be one, she lacks even half the strength needed to keep the citizens happy. The King and his army left our shores and what did she do? Took to the palace, retreated to her rooms… Wept.

How do you expect the people to react if our leaders cower so?

WATCHER: Well, I expect they were sad 'n all. Their husbands and sons left just like the Queen's did.

ADVISOR: And now you see the crux of the matter! A sad Kingdom can hardly be administered to achieve grandness! Many times I proposed to the Queen that *I* might speak to the people on her behalf, that I might rouse their hearts and make them proud to fight the thieving Trojans who took/

WATCHER: /they didn't take nothin' of ours though! I ain't even convinced they did take her, perhaps

Helen just left Menalaus for love, for Paris?
They do say he's pretty. A favourite of
Aphrodite.

ADVISOR: You prattle about things you know nothing
about. Paris spat in the face of all the great
houses, of which ours is the most grand. Our
King could not let his brother's wife run off as
though she were a weaver. You sound just like
Clytemnestra, talking about love and
Aphrodite.

WATCHER: Well the lack o' the men has made the whole
place feel sombre. I think she's got a point!
They shouldn't have gone.

ADVISOR: It's not the lack of men in general. Just the lack
of the one that matters. Now straighten up and
look smart, our Queen approaches.

CLYTEMNESTRA,
Queen of Mycenae,
approaches to join the WATCHER.

She does this often, joining the nightly vigil.

*She doesn't know why
she needs to be here tonight,
but she could not stay away.*

*The ADVISOR gives the two of them some space…
Uninterested in the mutterings of women.*

*CLYTEMNESTRA's words and tone are cold,
but the WATCHER is undeterred.*

*They have developed a form of friendship,
these 10 years watching for a beacon light.*

*And here,
away from the rest of the city,
they can speak more
freely.*

WATCHER: Clytemnestra, it's been years, you really think he's going to come back?

CLYTEMNESTRA: The gods will likely bring him back; he has too much to answer for here.

WATCHER: You only need a heads up that he's coming back so you can get all your crap hidden and warn lover-boy. Really you want bad news to come; if he has run off properly you can rule Mycenae freely.

CLYTEMNESTRA: Would you be silent?

WATCHER: 'Course, I wouldn't blame you for hating him and sleeping with his cousin after what he did to your daughter. I know the gods demanded it, but sacrificing her for the good of the fleet, when she was a good, and loyal daughter...

CLYTEMNESTRA: The gods had taken so much from my family, and still they demanded more. When a god asks you to… Well. I was sure we could have found another way… Perhaps we could have sacrificed him instead.

Every breath of wind since that day carries her screams to my ears, reminds me that her death cries filled the sails of his war ships. She was so small… so easily carried away.

WATCHER: Well, I've got bad news for you, then. I can see lights in the distance.

CLYTEMNESTRA: What?! But we're not ready! You're sure, you're certain that the beacon is lit?

WATCHER: As sure as I am that you're my Queen, when have these eyes ever let you down?

CLYTEMNESTRA: You're not as young as you once were, and I need this to be perfect, or you'll be wishing you'd been sacrificed instead. Advisor!

The ADVISOR bustles over,
irritated at being treated this way.

But,
he knows,
he cannot openly rebel.

The WATCHER goes on...

WATCHER: No, I'm not as young as I was, but my only job these long years has been to keep my eyes peeled, and that I did. He's on his way back; the King'll be back before you know it.

CLYTEMNESTRA: It's about time! Well get a move on, back to the palace, you can stop watching the horizon now. Advisor, make sure everything is as it should be. I want red carpets, I want the chefs woken, I want music, flowers, everything. He's on his way back.

ADVISOR: Oh no no, Clytemnestra, you must be mistaken. Just because there are pretty lights in the distance doesn't mean he's on his way back. Must you go to all this trouble just because of some shepherd's campfire?

CLYTEMNESTRA: Yes, thank you kindly for explaining that to me. I do have some wits about me, and as the Queen I'll do as I please.

> I placed that beacon there myself. It's one in a long chain from Troy, which allows news to travel quickly across great distances. Gods permitting, they'll return shortly.

Not entirely convinced but continuing to play the game, the ADVISOR chooses to accept this.

And so he twists the knife.

ADVISOR: Well, thank Zeus! And may Hades punish that slut Helen for allowing Paris to take her to curséd Troy. She brought it all upon them. The terrible cost of all those lives, all those urns packed smooth with the ashes of our men… And now they bring that death back to our shores when we so desperately needed life, and energy.

CLYTEMNESTRA: Would you concentrate on what's important here? Where is the sense of urgency, your King is on his way back and here you are, all stood around!

ADVISOR: If we're unsure as to how soon they will be here, is there any need for you to become this frantic?

CLYTEMNESTRA: Do as I say! I don't want anyone thinking I would do anything less than my duty.

If this is not absolutely perfect, I will hold you responsible. Go!

With a clear order received, the ADVISOR leaves.
CLYTEMNESTRA watches him go, making sure
he's well out of earshot
before speaking again to the WATCHER.

CLYTEMNESTRA: That one is far too loyal to my husband. I'll caution you not to put any trust in him, but I cannot deny he will help put the king at ease. We can't risk creating suspicion for him when he first steps onto the shore. I need him to think everything is as it should be, that I'm still his dutiful, passive, wife.

CLYTEMNESTRA is unable to hold back her disgust
at those words.
Of all, especially…

'wife'.

WATCHER: I'm at your disposal as always. I know you've got a cunning plan, I can see you have. What are you thinking?

CLYTEMNESTRA: A royal celebration of course, fit for His Majesty, the returning conqueror. Arrogant son of his mother, thinks he can go for a ten year siege before bursting back here as though nothing has changed? I'll make it seem like nothing has.

CLYTEMNESTRA and the WATCHER leave.
The night is full of preparations and apprehensions.

Dawn comes along
with AGAMEMNON's ship.
For the first time in ten years, we see AGAMEMNON
on Grecian soil.

The ADVISOR hovers
just behind his right elbow;
CASSANDRA trails behind.

This is not her home,
not her people,
not her place.

In silence she prays
that if she's quiet enough,
they'll forget about her.

Driven to secure his propaganda immediately.
AGAMEMNON and the ADVISOR scheme.

AGAMEMNON: Nothing compares to being home! I could kiss every rock and tree, I'm that happy to be back at my home, my birthplace. I tell you, it's a relief that I don't have to dodge death on foreign soil every waking moment. Perhaps I will get to die peacefully in my bed. Success is all the sweeter here, my triumph greater.

ADVISOR: My ever exalted Lord, Agamemnon... The people will be so pleased you've returned. It could not be better news for the common folk. They've grown restless, *leaderless* without their magnificent King. I fear you've left one battlefield to return to another.

AGAMEMNON: Nothing could be as dreadful as the battlegrounds of Troy. No man alive should count the dead, or wade through bodies and see their friends.

> But, whatever this new chapter brings, it starts with my success and bravery and will be talked about for a long time to come.

ADVISOR: Oh of course, of course. Ever so courageous of you, it's a surprise we managed even as well as we did, without your leadership.

AGAMEMNON: And let's not forget all the Trojan gold and glory I brought back with me, that will only give us better standing in the region. Something I'm sure we sorely need after being ruled by a woman for these long years.

ADVISOR: Well, we simply couldn't have done without you going to Troy, the new wealth you've brought will save the people from the brink of starvation. You *had* to leave.

AGAMEMNON: No one but I could have done it.

ADVISOR: Oh no, no one but you could have done it.

AGAMEMNON: We would never have gone just to retrieve a woman. There was a bigger picture... no, a grander plan!

ADVISOR: To save us.

AGAMEMNON: To save you.

The two of them share a look.
A brazen look,
of those who know their lies
will become the people's truth.

ADVISOR: I'll make sure the people aren't under any false impressions, of course. Anyone spreading lies will be dealt with, my Lord.

AGAMEMNON: See to it, we can't have them thinking anything but the best. There ought to be a celebration of my return. I didn't conquer Troy and burn it to the ground, sail all the way back across the seas, carrying mountains of riches to be met by just my advisor.

The façade appears to crack, a kingly tantrum brewing.

> I destroyed everything that was worthless in Troy, crushed under my superior battle prowess! Not even a temple or altar is left, it's all been flattened into the ground. The only things left of Troy are on my ship, and my wife does not come to greet me?!

ADVISOR: Of course there should be revelling! I believe the Queen is organising something suitable…

They have arrived at city streets now, where AGAMEMNON'S people are rejoicing.

CLYTEMNESTRA appears, flanked by a retinue of women, the WATCHER among them.

Plastering a smile to her face, CLYTEMNESTRA performs a saccharine pantomime of a happy reunion. They don't stop the parade, all the while getting nearer and nearer to the palace.

She addresses the crowd, barely looking at AGAMEMNON.

CLYTEMNESTRA: Oh I've waited so long for this day!
You would think this man had suffered
gruelling injury and endless plights to have
been away so long from his ever faithful *wife*.

Who but me could have kept strength and hope
that he would return, when only word of his
falls and pains reached my ears?

AGAMEMNON catches her arm and pulls him to her side. He's already sick of this.

AGAMEMNON: Yes, hello Clytemnestra.

She goes on without acknowledging him.

CLYTEMNESTRA: Oh indeed the days have been long
and the hours longer while I was parted from
my beloved husband. It was torture beyond
measure that I then was also forced to send our
baby boy away, for fear my countenance give
him leave for erratic moods and impulsive

behaviours. I shall be ever more glad that I can
send for him to return home also.

AGAMEMNON remembers where he is.
He can play this game too.

AGAMEMNON: Not surprised you had to send Orestes
away, nothing could tame that boy, just like his
father. Yes yes, get him home, now there's a
man around we'll be able to curb some of that
rebellious nature.

CLYTEMNESTRA: Of course, silly me... Just a woman,
unable to control him.

ADVISOR: Having the Prince return will certainly please
the people, my Lord. They will be eager to see
your family restored, just as theirs are being.

AGAMEMNON: See it done. There will be time enough to
speak about the people and the future; for now
we are celebrating my impressive - but well
deserved - victory. I've brought you back lots
of pretty things, Clytemnestra, like the finest

silk thread! Your embroidery will be the talk of all the Grecian queens.

CLYTEMNESTRA: I don't want silk thread, I wanted my husband.

She tries to drift away from his side a little, smiling but working hard to keep it there.

AGAMEMNON: I missed your company too. Come here, hug me properly. We've got time together now, don't we? I'll be here to run things and you can focus on being a better mother to our son and daughters.

CLYTEMNESTRA stiffens as AGAMEMNON pulls her hard into a staged embrace.

Her lips pass by his ear,
She fills one word with the hatred she feels for him,
whispering it,
as they break apart.

CLYTEMNESTRA: Daughter.

*The word is piercing, but he can't let anyone see the bolt
skewering his heart, barbs backwards.
This word can't be pulled from him.
The damage,
long ago done.*

*If he had hoped for the only other parent of their child
to show him she understood
what that decision had cost... well.*

*He raises his voice, his arms.
He calls to his people for love instead.*

AGAMEMNON: Whatever you want from all the spoils of Troy is yours, don't say I'm not good to you! Smile for me, Clytemnestra. You can be just as pretty as Helen when you try.

CLYTEMNESTRA: My Lord, there's much to do to celebrate your return, greeting the lords and unloading the ship...

AGAMEMNON: They can wait a moment until I've sacrificed to the gods, stop fussing and fretting,

I'll soon have things in order again. You won't have to stress yourself with these official matters anymore. We got home safe, and never again will something like that happen to this good house.

She stares, our CASSANDRA, at this so-called king.
So casually he mentions her name,
her name as if it held no meaning.

Her name, the rallying call on both sides,
her name, the last happy thing Paris ever said.

Her name, the woman who came to Troy for love, and brought only ruin.

Her name, her name, her name…

CASSANDRA: Helen meant death.

CLYTEMNESTRA: Pardon?

CASSANDRA: Her name. It means death.

I don't see goodness here either. Acts of evil only breed more evil, and houses create their own legacies. Yours didn't start very well. But, neither did mine.

CASSANDRA is unmoored; she is other, she is the prophetess.

Life goes on around her
—or maybe without her
—apart from her.

Reality has fractured
and we end up in her realm
beyond the water's edge.

The scene begins to change.
A moment caught in time,
a happy family eating dinner together.

This… is only for us.

CASSANDRA: I remember my first vision vividly. Sat at the dinner table, our brother Paris was boasting, nothing unusual there. He'd been going on and on about how he was destined to have the most beautiful woman there ever was. She would be his forever, their love would make history, and he would travel across the sea to get her.

APOLLO comes again.
Again unbidden, always unbidden, his arrival jarring like a beam of light when the curtain is drawn back too quickly,
stabbing into eyes that are used to the shade.

He comes only for CASSANDRA,
he comes only to be obeyed.

APOLLO: Don't let the ship leave.

CASSANDRA: I didn't understand where that voice had come from, or even what it was saying. What ship? No one was talking about any ship, or boat, or even a dingy. I ignored it.

The very idea of a mortal ignoring him, a god?
Of this mortal ignoring him?
She could never do it, he knows.

APOLLO reminds her.

Taunting, teasing, testing.

APOLLO: Don't ignore me, it's not very polite.

CASSANDRA: There's nothing to ignore, a voice in my head is just madness, and you won't make me spout insanities.

The mood has turned in an instant, a flash of anger, feigning hurt.

APOLLO: Make you? Make you? It's my gift, don't fight me Cassie!

*Behind her, her happy family freezes in motion, CASSANDRA alone
and scared, again.*

*She's cut off,
separated,
isolated... except from him.*

CASSANDRA: Time stood still in that moment, and silence filled the mouths of everyone around me. I wouldn't wish that feeling on anyone, that powerlessness. I struggled against it, to rise above the cold water and take a breath, but something I couldn't identify had me by my ankles, my wrists, my neck.

APOLLO &
CASSANDRA: DON'T LET THE SHIP LEAVE!

CASSANDRA: It forced its way up and out of me, using my voice to send its utterly terrifying message. It swelled and grew, and as it grew it became more hideous, torturous.

After that it was like someone had drawn the curtains on my eyes. I no longer had even a semblance of control as I fitted, making horrifying gurgling sounds and foaming at the mouth. My mother's guards held me under my arms and dragged me from the table, which had fallen into a silence so heavy my feet could be heard against the floor, I'm told.

To my bed, then. Locked up in my room as rumours of my madness spread, mostly thanks

to my brothers and sisters. I wouldn't eat; I
didn't want to feed that voice, feed its power
over me.

I could only see darkness out of the windows
no matter what time of day I looked. It was a
comfort to go mad, rather than face what was
happening to me, what I was being forced to
say.

I had many visitors: my mother, stoic, my
father, concerned, and endless streams of
siblings that wanted to poke the spectacle. None
of them helped.

Apollo came to me, and I thought that would be
the end of my story then and there. I don't
know what drove him to do it, but he helped.
He taught me how to resurface back to the land
of everyone else. Through gentle touches,
coaxing, I saw the man, or god, that I had
grown to care for once.

Perhaps it was to show me just what I'd done,
how much I could have learnt from him if I'd
just accepted this gift. If I'd done what he'd
wanted, he'd have taken care of me; I wouldn't
have had to go through this alone.

Or maybe, it was one of those acts of kindness he used to justify everything else. I don't believe it was for me at all.

The moment breaks suddenly, almost violently.
We are back in Mycenae.
The Royal retinue has arrived at the steps
before the palace's entrance,
a red carpet laid out.

The crowd have been pushed back behind barriers, though those closest could still hear if voices were raised.

CLYTEMNESTRA: My Lord, why don't we continue our discussion somewhere more private? I could get you a glass of wine...

AGAMEMNON halts in place, his voice lowered but a seething rage ripples beneath his mask.
CLYTEMNESTRA's smile stays in place better than his.

The ADVISOR is too close.

Neither AGAMEMNON nor CLYTEMNESTRA can say everything they'd like, but the veiled insults get a little less veiled, and cut a little closer to the bone.

AGAMEMNON: Clytemnestra what is this? I can't walk on a bloody red carpet after all the men have been through. Do you want me to anger the gods again? You should know better than any, the prices they ask when they're angered.

CLYTEMNESTRA: I've been waiting a long time for you to come home, but don't think I've forgotten what happened when you left. Some shaman tells you Artemis demands our daughter's death for you to sail safely, and you think it's necessary to murder our baby.

Why would I risk further anger from our vengeful deities? Why did I send Orestes away if I had so little sense?

AGAMEMNON: I just want to get inside. A red carpet is in poor taste no matter how you cut it. You think you're the only wife that's been through this?

*Grasping her chin, he tilts her face up,
forcing her to look into his eyes.*

A parody of romance for the watchful eyes,
but they cannot hear how he speaks.

AGAMEMNON: You're not special, Clytemnestra. I am a King amongst Kings but you are a consolation prize of a Queen.

That wasn't nearly as vicious as he could be in private.
He'd held back because of the crowd, she knew.

She'd use the crowd to her advantage, then.

CLYTEMNESTRA: You think Priam would have spared a moment before walking over a red carpet of your corpse? Please, we went to all this effort...

He glances at the ADVISOR, the WATCHER,
CASSANDRA,
and the crowds, seeing their restlessness.
The longer they linger at the steps without going inside...

AGAMEMNON drops his hand.
Irritation settles into him.

AGAMEMNON: I won't argue any more. You've got this silly notion in your head, I can see you won't relent and I don't want a scene in front of my own door.

But in return… look after Cassie for me. She's come a long way to keep me company. She's Priam's daughter too, so I won't have her treated any worse than you'd treat me.

CLYTEMNESTRA: You'll both get exactly the same. I don't have a choice about that now.

AGAMEMNON: You should be grateful not to have a choice. I'm here to relieve you of all that decision making pressure.

CLYTEMNESTRA: Things hardly fell into total disrepair during your absence. My choices have led us through 10 years.

AGAMEMNON: I understand you've done your best; it's not your fault. With my return, everything will soon be fixed.

*AGAMEMNON steps onto the red silk carpet,
and the world changes.*

Before us, before CASSANDRA,

*CLYTEMNESTRA takes this carpet,
and with it, the very symbol of AGAMEMNON's hubris,
she will end his life.*

A drumbeat sounds, or is it a heartbeat?

*The death is gruesome, performed gracefully and forcefully,
some moments lighting quick and others
lingering far beyond comfort.*

*CASSANDRA is overcome, on her knees,
unable to look away, unable to do anything
even if she wanted to.*

*The drums go on, faster and faster, AGAMEMNON
struggling, clinging to life as
CLYTEMNESTRA stands above him,
bathed in red.*

*A crescendo.
A corpse.*

Silence as the body is dragged from sight,
the carpet drawn along behind
as if it were a trail of blood.

Even though this vision is over, this power is APOLLO's
and it's viscid on the air, in our mouths.
This time it's hard to swim back to reality's shores.

And though he cannot have witnessed this
the ADVISOR's thumbs are pricking.

ADVISOR: It's most peculiar. I had hoped with my Lord's return we would all feel better, and Clytemnestra certainly seems pleased to have her husband back.

But, I can't help but feel a vast sense of doom upon my shoulders; anxiety fills me with doubt.

A call comes from out of sight, fit and healthy.

AGAMEMNON: Advisor! My ships need unloading!

The ADVISOR hurries to his King, leaving us.

CLYTEMNESTRA is as she was before, by no means happy but not the woman who just killed in a bloody rage. Frustrated to be left to handle CASSANDRA, she gestures sharply for her to enter the house.

The WATCHER, curious, listens in.

CLYTEMNESTRA: Come on now, get inside, I can't have you dawdling on the steps or people will talk. Mycenae might not be like Troy, but I've been bid "spare no comfort or expense" on you. I'll have the maids ready a room close to my husband's, he will want to make certain you're *cared* for.

CASSANDRA is still gripped by the terror of her vision, unable to speak, unable to do more than stand and shake her head, shake her whole body with tremors.

CLYTEMNESTRA rolls her eyes, looking back to the WATCHER for her thoughts on this oddly behaving girl.

WATCHER: Perhaps her Greek isn't very good?

CLYTEMNESTRA: No, that's not it, *he* wouldn't hold with idiots. Besides, she's a princess of Troy. She'd have been taught many persuasive arts so she could be the perfect pet for a prince. Before she became a priestess, of course.

WATCHER: Do you see something I don't?

CLYTEMNESTRA: Constantly. Look at the way she's dressed! You've seen our priestesses dressed similarly, haven't you?

WATCHER: Just thought that was what they liked wearing, thought it were cold in the temples or somethin'.

CLYTEMNESTRA: It's a wonder I keep you around. No, she's a foreign princess who chose to serve the gods. Speaking in tongues won't be an issue for her, probably whispering nasty things in my husband's ear.

WATCHER: Good job my family have been serving yours for 'undreds o' years or I recon you woulda got rid of me an' all. But look 'ere, why do you care what she's been saying, or not saying by the way things are going, to the King?

CLYTEMNESTRA: It's just one more thing I have to take care of! And to have kept me waiting for ten years only to return with one of them, one of the enemy's sluts to our beautiful kingdom is abhorrent.

> Ugh, never mind, it's useless explaining to you. She's probably just caught up inside her own head. No good comes from women feeling themselves important, when all they have comes from the gods.

This irritated mention of the gods stirs CASSANDRA.
It's been hardest for her, of all, to shake off the terror.
Slowly as if waking from sleep,
she comes back to the world.

These two women stand
either side of a gulf of understanding.

CASSANDRA is caught between her desire to live

and her understanding of CLYTEMNESTRA's anger.

CLYTEMNESTRA is caught between her hatred of AGAMEMNON, and her knowledge that it isn't CASSANDRA's fault her daughter is dead.

CASSANDRA: All I have, and my tragedy too. The gods… ah, just one god, has brought me here.

CLYTEMNESTRA: You're hardly acting like a deranged captive who's here against her will. Where are your screams, your fight? Why do you look as though you've given up?

    Rumours have reached us here, Cassandra, of how you thought yourself better than Apollo. Your hubris brought you here, and you've taken my King with you.

CASSANDRA: What would you have done in my place? You have no idea what led me to that point, to the moment where I refused Apollo one thing, one thing! When I had already given everything else...

CLYTEMNESTRA: Don't act like you didn't walk into this, *princess*. If he were as awful as all your whining suggests, you could have let him take one of the other girls! But no, you thought yourself beautiful enough to have been loved by a god, and didn't like that these things always come with a cost.

CASSANDRA: You were a young girl once, and you may have a fair memory of how that felt. But you also have the luxury of hindsight, memories of your younger self where you look back and scream 'what were you thinking?'

We're almost always thinking the same things, more or less. This is how everyone else is, this will make me happy, this is where I'm safe, this will win me love or acclaim or money or power.

We're taught modesty is the goal and so we learn to hate ourselves in order to make it true. We're expected to line up along the side of the hall and wait to be noticed, wait for someone to *insist* we are all they could ever want. Little girls dream of their soulmates, of someone that loves them so much they can't stand to be apart.

APOLLO approaches with unhurried strides.
More of a man this time, he is gentle with CASSANDRA
and this vision mirrors him. We are coaxed in.

Surreal serenity.
CASSANDRA and APOLLO sit together on a date
as a couple might.

APOLLO: You're so beautiful. You know, no one else sees you like I do.

CASSANDRA: Apollo, honestly, stop it. I'm nothing special, I really don't know why you've chosen me out of all people.

APOLLO: Eh, you were the first I'd seen that day, and seemed happy to play along with me.

CASSANDRA: Oh…

APOLLO: I'm kidding! Don't take what I say so seriously, honestly you think I'd just pick anyone? That's

not fair. I've just told you how beautiful you
are.

CASSANDRA: I'm sorry, I didn't mean to upset you, it
just wasn't obvious to me it was a joke.
You're too good at hiding your feelings.

APOLLO: And why do you think that is?

This silence is loaded, dangerous.

CASSANDRA the deer
in the crosshairs of APOLLO's piercing eyes,
his temper stoked.

APOLLO: You drive me crazy, why won't you let me take
you away from here? It's my temple, you're
supposed to want to run away with me.

CASSANDRA: I… My friends…

APOLLO: Won't miss you, they barely even notice you…
It makes me so angry seeing how they treat

you. You know they're more concerned with how the fasting is going or whether it's hubris to wear makeup.

They're not like you, not like us. They don't get it the way we do, and it's maddening to think of all the time you're stuck in there. I just want you all to myself. I love you.

CASSANDRA: They're not that bad! And besides, I can't just up and leave my family either, I've got responsibilities here.

APOLLO: Cassie... I said I love you.

CASSANDRA: I love you too, but we were talking about leaving/

APOLLO: /You don't love me, Cassie, you don't. Or else you'd come with me as I ask! Why can't you see how much I'm doing for you?

Gone is the man; the god APOLLO exits brusquely,

aiming to hurt.

CASSANDRA tries desperately to placate him, to no end.

*The barrier between reality and
CASSANDRA weakens again.*

*More of APOLLO spills out onto those around.
CLYTEMNESTRA, unable to do anything else,
steps into the silence APOLLO leaves behind.*

CLYTEMNESTRA: You let yourself be sweet talked into a position you didn't want to be in. You didn't think things through and you got your comeuppance. This is your fault.

CASSANDRA: You can't tell me you've never let someone talk you into doing something you didn't want to do. That's called compromising.

But some people expect to get their way more times than their share. We call these people bossy, or say they're using guilt to get their way. They're not clever, or subtle.

CLYTEMNESTRA: Exactly, and so you avoid them, or hold your ground.

CASSANDRA: And then there are manipulators, true manipulators. They are so very good at what they do. So good at taking something oh so naive and turning it into their plaything.

They don't start straight away, they take their time. They get to know you, to understand you and how you react. How does a raised voice affect you? Do you shout back? Yes? They'll try something else. You freeze, you want it to stop, you'll do anything to make it stop? Congratulations, now they know they can shout you into agreeing not to make them angry any more.

CLYTEMNESTRA: Oh please, without a victim, 'manipulators' would have to learn to play nicely. Stop shirking your share of the blame here, Cassandra.

CASSANDRA: I had friends like you who told me to see sense, who told me this wasn't healthy. But I defended him. He said they just wanted to split us apart, that they were jealous, or they didn't understand. And he would be so, so unbelievably hurt. He loved me, and yet I would listen to them say bad things about him? How could I believe them over him?

My friends couldn't know everything about us, didn't I know him, know better? They could only go off what I was saying about him. So, I stopped talking to them in case I gave them a worse impression of him.

I was taught not to trust anyone except him, not even my own thoughts. Every day that someone told me he was bad for me was a day that he was proved right.

CLYTEMNESTRA: I have to applaud your convoluted perspective, even if it is pathetic.

CASSANDRA: Fight this, Clytemnestra! Oh, great Queen, you who have ruled alone.

You would still rather ignore me than face the truth? You could have *been* me. All women suffer under the same bondage, it's just that some restraints are made of gold.

Are yours? Were your daughter's?

Use your rage to fight for us. It's not too late.
Be a sword to cut through the chains, not
another jailbird in her own ornate cage.

CLYTEMNESTRA: That's where you and I are different.
The time where I cared about anyone other than
myself ended the day I saw the warships leave,
their sails plump with my daughter's dying
screams. Naivety is a luxury, *Cassandra*, and
you have had your fair share of luxury in life.
Perhaps this is all you deserve.

I'm done. If Agamemnon left you out here
alone, I will too. Come in when you want, I
have plans for you both.

CLYTEMNESTRA leaves, her heart shut.

CASSANDRA paces for a little while,
her tenuous connection with reality wavering.

Could CLYTEMNESTRA have been swayed not to kill her,
if she'd said the right words?
If she did, would that have spared AGAMEMNON?

How would she have felt if that was so?

*The WATCHER, who up 'til now
had been keeping out of it,
sidles over and tries to engage with CASSANDRA.*

*But when CASSANDRA speaks,
she slips between addressing this world and
that other place,
her feet on the edge of a cliff we cannot see.*

WATCHER: I think she's being a little harsh on you, but
you did come back on the arm of her King,
enough to make anyone feel the worst for you.

CASSANDRA: Plans for us both, she says. Oh Apollo,
how could you do this to me?

WATCHER: Mighty fine weather today, bet you're loving
being on dry land again, huh?

CASSANDRA: I had hoped never to take a step on to the
boat in the first place! I had hoped, when they
were sacking my city, that I would end up

amongst the dead. A quick end, an end fit for a warrior and not a prize. Or, that I could stay with my people, not forced onto a ship and taken to a land I don't recognise, so far away from anything and everything I've ever known.

But that's not the way of war, is it? Your King threw many a tantrum and because of it, the Greeks made me into an object, a foreign souvenir gifted to him.

You know, in between Ajax and Agamemnon, I was left in a makeshift cell that had been put together on the beach? They'd got quite good at building these things over the ten years, in between slaughtering and squabbling. Alone, for the first time since my city had fallen, I thought about how I could take back possession of my life from them. One final act of defiance, my suicide. I had a rope, and a beam, and a rock I could jump from…

WATCHER: Oh! You didn't!

CASSANDRA: I'm still here, am I not?! The beam snapped and the sound brought the soldiers. I wasn't given another opportunity.

WATCHER: The gods sure like you then don't they? Aren't you grateful they didn't let you do something that silly now!

CASSANDRA: I had thought it meant Apollo was ready to give me another chance, that he was saving me for something better, a reason. I made them go back for the dress he gave me, the jewellery. I prayed and prayed for him to forgive me, though now I'm not even sure what I wanted forgiveness for. Maybe he'd grant me an opportunity to fix whatever it was I'd done and earn back my life…

But really he was just saving me for this! An even worse fate than the one I thought I'd been handed. This, gods forsaken, vile house.

You would bring me to this house, to a place where father murders daughter, where son will murder mother. You just wanted to stand in front of me, lead me step by step to this house where the occupants bathe in blood. A new disaster happens here today, and yet help stands too far away. And you think I deserve it! Whatever did I do?!

WATCHER: I don't think you're well, perhaps you've got a touch of sunstroke on the ship…

CASSANDRA: Sunstroke. One way of putting it.

WATCHER: Well out with it, what did you mean, about this house?

CASSANDRA: When I was small, I would play along the riverbank. I was cherished by the sun god, his affection for me becoming ever stronger. Slowly as I grew, I grew to love him back, and for a time we were together. He was all I'd known, grooming me to be his. He used to say, he didn't have to guide me much, I flourished as if I'd known his desires from birth. I didn't hear how that sounded, or if I did I didn't mind back then… Those were the happiest days of my life.

With his sweet breath came prophecies, yet before too long I could no longer be what he wanted, no longer could I only obey and never question... But the gift had already been given. From then on, no one has believed me.

WATCHER: The who now?

CASSANDRA: The Lord Apollo holds the gift of prophecy. He gave me the ability to see the future.

WATCHER: Great! Oooh, tell me what happens to Mycenae!

CASSANDRA: You don't actually want to know. And it wouldn't help you escape it.

WATCHER: Escape what, what?

CASSANDRA: Your city will fall to ruins just like mine, and all because of your royals, because you can't stop blaming women for your men's mistakes. Helen - slut. Clytemnestra - power-hungry, bitch. Never Paris - a thief, Agamemnon - an abuser.

WATCHER: All right love, I only really wanted news about the rain or the harvest. Harvest would be best to know I reckon. Will the apples be alright? Missed them last year, could have done with a good apple pie…

CASSANDRA: This is agony! I tell you there will be death here, a husband, his blood in the bath and treachery in a woman's heart. And yet you still don't believe me. How can your Queen call me prophetess, but you still can't see I tell the truth?

WATCHER: You have been called a seer, I grant you. And I'm not sure how you could have been confident about Troy falling after it stood for ten years. But after that you lose me, the King is home and safe.

CASSANDRA: You shall see Agamemnon dead and me alongside.

WATCHER: Never say that again.

CASSANDRA: Death is coming for me, I can see it. I can feel it, in the very walls of *this house* and every, single, second, of my life since *you* has led to it.

Apollo enough, enough now, please! You've brought me here, to die, a poison for me and a blade for him, so even my death will be slow, and painful. How can one slight, one error in your eyes, justify you punishing my life and determining my very death too?

I won't do this. Take back your trinkets, your presents, your small gifts and the big. I won't wear your dress or your jewellery, I will go as me to this petty revenge.

WATCHER: Ain't no one here except me, love. And you might want to mind yourself spouting all that around their royal majesties! Come on, best you get inside now.

The WATCHER ushers her along, mothering and kind, but clearly thinking the girl is mad.

Chaos seems to be creeping in

gone are the careful moments
choreographed for public viewing
in their place, frantic energy.

CLYTEMNESTRA returns,
no longer as poised or composed as before.

CLYTEMNESTRA: Oh, where did she go? You've not let her run off to the gods, have you?

WATCHER: Who?

CLYTEMNESTRA: The girl, the stupid Trojan girl my repulsive husband brought back to parade in my face!

WATCHER: Oh, I sent her off to the master's room, figured you'd be… catching up with him yourself.

CLYTEMNESTRA: Obviously not.

WATCHER: What's got you so riled? Not like you weren't having your fun while he was away.

CLYTEMNESTRA: It's not like he left me on some work weekend away, he left me for ten years! You leave your wife for ten years, and then flounce home with a foreign floozy, see if that goes well. It's one thing not to try to make amends and another to rub salt into the wound of our marriage.

WATCHER: She's just some girl who don't make no sense. Not you, is she? And he came home to you.

CLYTEMNESTRA: He came home to his kingdom. And she's not some commoner girl, she's a foreign princess, possibly the only heir to the Trojan throne left. I won't be unseated by that little creature. She should have died in Troy rather than take a step into my kingdom!

WATCHER: Maybe our Lord is more Trojan now than Greek, that's why he likes her.

*Across the palace grounds
CASSANDRA and AGAMEMNON,
already in his rooms.*

*Here he isn't concerned. He's home,
in control, his things don't slide across
the mudslicked tent floor,
his men, only his, guard the palace.*

*No gods blessed sons of other gods
or whining pampered princes pleading for their homes
no screamed curses from hospital beds.*

*One little princess, alone.
Younger than that insipid wife of his
but much too talkative.*

CASSANDRA: They found me when I was small, me and my brother, in the temple of Phoebus Apollo with two serpents licking at our ears. The snakes were driven off of course, but it was a sign. A sign! They all said so. What was more natural than enlisting me to become a priestess of Apollo, I who was so favoured?

AGAMEMNON: Wine?

CASSANDRA: No, thank you.

*AGAMEMNON pours two glasses anyway.
It didn't matter what she said.*

CASSANDRA: I said no.

AGAMEMNON: And I didn't listen, you'll get the hang of it.

CASSANDRA: Over your dead body.

AGAMEMNON: Cassie, why don't you ever make things easier on yourself?

CASSANDRA: What does it matter? You didn't want to drown at sea, and yet you will die here at the hands of a woman I can't blame. You probably treated her vilely when you controlled her. She's learnt she's the one that has control now, and so you turn to me instead.

AGAMEMNON: I don't understand any of your babbling, and you're right, I don't much care. Come here, come to me.

CASSANDRA: No, thank you.

AGAMEMNON shucks off any remaining civility like a coat or boots, discarding it without a thought.

He's had to control himself with CLYTEMNESTRA but gone are those restraints now, here, with CASSANDRA.

AGAMEMNON: You think you're better than everyone else, is that it? I don't think you understand how much I've done for you. It's not every girl that walked away from Troy. I could have left you to the rest of my men, *they* wouldn't have been as nice as I am.

CASSANDRA: I'm supposed to thank you for not killing me along with my family? You haven't saved

me from your men, you've just changed my
captor from them to yourself.

AGAMEMNON: You're an ungrateful witch who used her
way with words to scare everyone around you.
It won't work on me. I know you're enjoying
this, the power trip. Every woman wants to be
noticed, desired, and by a powerful man no
less.

CASSANDRA: You'd have been right about me, about
that, once. After I'd been inducted into the
temple, my status as his favourite was quickly
made known. All my omens were favourable.
Any opportunity he had to show us that I was
his, he took.

Even during periods of drought, the flowers on
my window stayed blooming, the sun always
shone on my rest days, nothing went wrong for
me and I revelled in it. I *loved* it.

I doubt you would know what it felt like, you
who have always been the most important
person in whatever room you've entered. It felt
incredible. It was my own form of power, it
was intense and all consuming, it was… awful.

You powerful men! You're right to say the attentions that you give to the weak are often desired, but only at first! That intensity... you burn so bright, and even though cold people gather around a fire, the licking flame still burns when you're too close. Why can't you understand/

AGAMEMNON: /Now you're just complaining because you couldn't handle everything you asked for, you're pathetic.

CASSANDRA: Agamemnon, hear me, please. Your wife is planning your murder right now and it's because of your pride. Let me go, we don't both have to die here.

AGAMEMNON: No one is dying! I'm sick of your blathering, I liked it better when you were silent. What possible danger could I be in, that I didn't face a thousand times over before? I didn't come all the way home to imagine a new battle, Cassie.

CASSANDRA: I'm not Cassie, your pet princess! I am the prophetess Cassandra and you know I saw the fall of Troy...

AGAMEMNON: I know your own people thought you were an attention seeking harpy with nothing better to do than be a harbinger of doom. There'll be none of that self-pitying nonsense here, do you understand?

CASSANDRA: I understand more than you do; I hope the Queen makes your death slow.

AGAMEMNON: I warned you, I am the King. Come over here now, *Cassie*!

APOLLO comes to CASSANDRA,
drawing her into his arms.

They begin to dance while she speaks
the dance starting sweetly
before becoming slowly more violent.

They remain in physical contact the whole time,
tethered, though as the dance goes on

*CASSANDRA tries again and again
to pull away.*

CASSANDRA: One night at the temple I'm trying to speak with the gods. The floor is cold, my knees ache, the others have collapsed or given up, but not me. I was the favoured one, I'd been chosen from birth to be here. I was so sure he'd come back to me that nothing could have moved me from that spot.

And finally, there, bathed in golden light, was my beloved Apollo. Just as I'd been told would happen if I prayed hard enough, if I begged him to forgive me. Radiant, the sun god with his bronzed skin and piercing, cold-sky coloured eyes. In that vision I dared to hope his attention would fall to me, that I could serve him better, that this time he wouldn't walk away from me.

Again we fell into the comforting rhythm of our 'love'. I tried so hard to always do what he asked, think of new ways to delight and surprise him. I was so scared he'd leave me again, and so unable to understand what I'd done wrong when I upset him. I'd invent new reasons for me to be at fault, to need to say sorry.

I forged a careful, and I thought happy, romance. But that wasn't what he wanted me for, and again I dared to refuse his physical intentions. When he couldn't overpower me as a man, I saw him transform into a wolf of fearsome proportions. Paralysed, it was that form that pinned me to the ground and that spat furiously into my mouth, leaving behind a loathsome, foul taste on my tongue.

What right had I to say no? Hadn't I wanted to serve? Wasn't it my purpose as priestess to allow him to possess me completely?

APOLLO's hands caress her throat, a strangling hold.

Finally, he casts her aside
their connection broken
CASSANDRA's heart,
broken.

APOLLO,
cold,
stands apart from her
but not gone.

APOLLO: You disappoint me, Cassie.

CASSANDRA: This is what pain is. Up until now I thought I knew what it meant to be in pain, but it's barely grazed me as it passed by.

AGAMEMNON,
distinctly unaffected by what's just occurred.

AGAMEMNON: I haven't hurt you, what are you talking about?

CASSANDRA: Not you, not this, I can name this pain. Apollo. The root and cause of every bruise and cut is Apollo, Apollo.

AGAMEMNON: You're blathering again.

APOLLO: Cassie. Come to me and I can make it stop, give you something else to think about, distract you from whatever pain you're feeling.

CASSANDRA: No, you can't! Because it's mine, my pain. Separate from losing my home and my family, this is only mine, and it feels like it could break me.

APOLLO: So let me take it away. Cassie, you know I can make you feel better, fix you. With a little work, you could be perfect for me.

CASSANDRA: I wish I could let you, it would be so easy. Head down, do what I'm told, never say no… Give up.

Perhaps I could fall into madness again instead. I wish I could break now and skip off happily to my death, ruin all your fun and enjoyment in it, make light of the fact a jilted ex has set-up my murder. But then we'd be back at square one, and I'd be voiceless again.

But if I don't give up then how do I go on? From moment to moment I feel myself becoming less and less who I was, continuously being shaped by your actions. Even now I can't be angry though I have every right. Even now, all I feel in here, is hurt.

I wasn't happy with you, but I'm not happy without you either. It just hurts in different ways. How do you protect against both?

I can't, is the answer. But now, here, presented with only the option of returning to you or how I die, I suppose all there is to do is to remember that no pain lasts forever. Even if it feels insurmountable, no one can feel an emotion of this magnitude without something changing, without mastering it, taking control of it, or letting it go.

APOLLO: Cassie…

*APOLLO stays long enough
to ensure the next chain of events begins
before slipping away.*

*AGAMEMNON, his mind closed to her
conversation with APOLLO
takes over the god's position in the dance
repeating it all over again.*

*The movements are sharp and controlled,
devoid of any of the tenderness APOLLO started with.
Forcing CASSANDRA to bend*

to his will this time.

CASSANDRA: And with Agamemnon we just go again and do the same. I shouldn't be surprised. I'm not surprised. I'm numb, and dumb, and done.

I let, but not consent it to happen because I can see the outcome of trying to break the cycle - the cyclic nature of the abused fighting back, of the abuser fighting harder, dirtier, longer, until shattered, broken, weeping I collapse into that familiar, predictable, deadly serenity of the normality of this.

To fight would prolong the stay, and I prefer this. What's a little pain to anguish, and what's a little rape from a king?

Throughout the war I was told this is part of being King, so is it really his fault? He is supposed to take home the young princess as spoils of war. He's rescuing me. Should I not be grateful for his attentions?

The moves repeat.

AGAMEMNON goes for CASSANDRA's throat.

He lingers longer,
rabid and monstrous,
before he too
discards her.

AGAMEMNON: I'm going to take a bath. You take a stroll in the gardens and I'll send my wife to show you the guest room.

CASSANDRA: Why not? Enjoy the bath.

Leaving CASSANDRA
to gather herself, we are pulled to the palace gardens.
The night is temperate, perfect for a walk before bed.

These gardens are beautiful, manicured.
There is nothing wild about them.
Every flower has its place.

The WATCHER comes to CLYTEMNESTRA's side.
The Queen is trying to quell her racing heart,
though with little success.

She knows what the plan is.
She knows what she's supposed to do next,

what she wants to do next.

*But wanting to do it
and going through with it
are two different things.*

*Could she really kill her husband?
Did she have enough nerve,
enough strength?*

APOLLO lurks behind, unseen.

WATCHER: My Lady, Agamemnon's told me to tell you to give that Cassandra a bedroom… He's in the bath you see.

CLYTEMNESTRA: Well, at least splitting them up means it'll be easier. I won't have to fight the girl while he's taking his last breaths.

WATCHER: Look, here, I know you're hell bent on this revenge thing, and like I said, it was a right ol' shame with your daughter, but he's the King, ain't he got a right to his own property?

CLYTEMNESTRA: You complete fool, you aren't understanding. Would you stop trying to compare this to a petty argument between a husband and a wife.

*APOLLO circles CLYTEMNESTRA,
his influence fuelling her anger.
AGAMEMNON is no king.
He isn't worth saving.*

CLYTEMNESTRA: I am a Queen, and the King has done me wrong. I've ruled this kingdom since he left, and now he's come back he'll take it away from me. He's as foreign as she is now; I will not let an invader robe me of my throne.

WATCHER: You might be right, I'm an old fool. If you'll just listen a little longer…

CLYTEMNESTRA: No! I have no need to listen - to anyone - ever again. I am monarch here and you will do what I say. Agamemnon dies.

Fate is such an easy thing to manipulate,

almost as easy as young girls.

Needing only one more nudge before
all the pieces fall
into place, into line.

APOLLO: And so does the whore.

CLYTEMNESTRA: And so does the whore.

APOLLO: She thinks she knows what's coming for her, and we wouldn't want to disappoint. She deserves it for defying me, doesn't she, Clytemnestra?

CLYTEMNESTRA: She deserves it for defying me.

WATCHER: This ain't right, this ain't you. Why'd the girl have to come in to it, when she's done nothing. Defied you? She's been his victim just as much as you!

APOLLO: She's come in your daughter's place, remember. A god took a princess from you, a god gave you one back.

CLYTEMNESTRA: He took my princess from me.

WATCHER: So you'll take her from him? Who wins there?

APOLLO: Me, of course.

CLYTEMNESTRA: Me, of course.

WATCHER: I won't be a part of it, my Queen, though I've served you faithfully otherwise.

CLYTEMNESTRA: Then go home. I've strength enough myself.

*APOLLO leads CLYTEMNESTRA away,
her feet unable to step off the path
he's put them on.*

AGAMEMNON's death is unavoidable.
Sorrow hits the WATCHER,
she stays in the garden, remains true to her words.

She has been unaffected by APOLLO's influence,
by strength of character…
Or him simply not thinking her important enough.

The WATCHER sees CASSANDRA approaching.
Seemingly unaware of the danger she's in,
CASSANDRA carries a single flower stem.

Her Queen might be mad,
but CLYTEMNESTRA had always done her best
for her people.

The WATCHER believed
in CLYTEMNESTRA.
But she cannot stand idly by
against CASSANDRA.

She must do something.

WATCHER: I'd get hung for this girl, but if I were you I'd make a run for it.

CASSANDRA: You're kind, but there's no place I could go to avoid this. It would be foolish, and I'd rather spend my last moments here, smelling the flowers with grass under my feet, rather than fighting with a guard.

WATCHER: Honestly I look at you and see you talking, but the words that come out must be Trojan. Just get on up the steps and you'll be out by my old post. Plenty of ways down to the docks there, nab a small boat and you'll be happy, free.

CASSANDRA: It's no use, I can see what would happen if I tried. I'd get to the boats alright, but then your Queen's guards would have sent burning arrows after me. If I get to pick a death, poison is better than fire.

WATCHER: I should have retired already, I'm getting too old for this girl.

CASSANDRA: I think, if I had been able to stay here, we'd have gotten through to each other. It's nice to have met you.

Kindness from hurt
no lashings from the whipped
vulnerability from a heart cut open.

This Trojan girl
whose world was stolen, broken, burned
hands the WATCHER her flower.

The gesture, simple.
The WATCHER, choked
with emotion accepts it gently, reverently.

WATCHER: Pretty sure everyone else is the fool, not me, these royal types. And I am sure I'm glad a god's never chosen me as their favourite. The grace of the gods, I'm pretty sure, is a grace that comes with violence.

The WATCHER slowly leaves,
unable to help and
unable to bear it.

CASSANDRA: Even without his presence, the roots of our conversations have buried down deep.

Signs and messages kept coming. Only after I'd left was he sorry, then angry, then I've hurt him... I've hurt him.

And the gift, never wanted, never asked for, festers and moulds. I want to claw him out of me. I want to cut off every bit of flesh that came into contact with him, I want to weed out the sickness that is him, that is me for letting it happen.

APOLLO steps into the light.
He is determined to make this hurt CASSANDRA as much as possible.

Truly he is the god of the Sun in this moment.

The sun that burns,
that blinds,
that travels across the sky unceasingly and eternally.

APOLLO: Cassie.

CASSANDRA: Don't. Call me that.

APOLLO: Cassie I was just mad… You really upset me, and after everything I'd done for you, you brought this on yourself.

CASSANDRA: No. No! People that love each other don't do this to each other. It's a lie. People that love each other put each other first!

APOLLO: Then I guess you didn't love me as much as I loved you. You were just too selfish to think of someone else.

CASSANDRA: You can say I'm the selfish one, that I never put you first, but that's you. Don't spin your revenge plan into something just, and righteous. You're a child throwing a tantrum because your plaything bit back, because I was a person with needs that were my own and not just a need to serve.

APOLLO: It's not revenge, it's justice. But I can save you from it, or make it easier. Just say you need me…

CASSANDRA: I'll never need your help again.

> Poisons need to be sucked out, but if they enter the bloodstream it's too late. If I can't find the *me* in the ruins of the remains, then what remains should be ruined, removed. I won't let you exist in me, even if that means I cannot exist. Who would I be, if I was still what you made?

He leaves, disgusted and disgusting.

CASSANDRA is alone, once again just as we found her.

Everywhere, always nowhere, never.

She breathes easier than she has in years.

This moment is hers.

CASSANDRA: I will meet this death.

> Whatever they say about things that don't kill you only make you stronger... That's not a

given. You don't get stronger just by virtue of not dying, or else where is the justice for the broken?

We have to allow people to break, to take time, to not be okay. They can build themselves up again, they can become stronger, they can push on and survive. But telling them that it just happens is not true. Whatever doesn't kill you, stays with you. You decide how it affects you.

If only I had time. I think I'd have worked through it and been one of the successes. I think…

Well, for once, I don't know. What a relief that is.

And now she comes, grieving mother and scorned lover, the archetype of an angry woman. How could anyone deny her this vengeance? Death to the child killer and death to his mistress. He talks about justice, well there is some in her being the one to do it. My end can be a beginning to someone else's story, not just a final blow from a spoilt god.

Slay me, Clytemnestra. End it. Hurry.

WITH THANKS

All characters are shaped by those who tread the boards in their guise, all scripts are guided by those that support dreams.

CASSANDRA - Lyna Dubarry

APOLLO - Hayden Tyler, Thomas Devlin

CLYTEMNESTRA - Beth Asher, Anne Hayward

AGAMEMNON - Paul Irwin, Thomas Devlin

THE WATCHER - Jade Clulee, Forest Morgan

THE ADVISOR - Hiral Varsani, Tommy Campe

DIRECTOR - Ollie Harrington

LX DESIGN & TECHNICIAN - Lauren Flynn

MUSIC COMPOSER - Josh Gardner

PHOTOGRAPHY - Caitlin MacNamara

COLLABORATORS - Blue Elephant Theatre, Hellenic Society

THE ORIGINAL BLUE ELEPHANT PERFORMANCE

JUNE 2018

CASSANDRA

Lyna Dubarry

Caitlin MacNamara - Photography

CLYTEMNESTRA & THE ADVISOR
Beth Asher & Hiral Varsani

Caitlin MacNamara - Photography

CLYTEMNESTRA, AGAMEMNON & CASSANDRA

Beth Asher, Lyna Dubarry & Paul Irwin

Caitlin MacNamara – Photography

CASSANDRA & AGAMEMNON
Paul Irwin & Lyna Dubarry

Caitlin MacNamara – Photography

CASSANDRA & APOLLO

Lyna Dubarry & Hayden Tyler

Caitlin MacNamara – Photography

THE WATCHER & CASSANDRA
Jade Clulee & Lyna Dubarry

Caitlin MacNamara - Photography

CASSANDRA

Lyna Dubarry

Caitlin MacNamara - Photography

www.ingramcontent.com/pod-product-compliance
Lightning Source LLC
Chambersburg PA
CBHW071215070526
44584CB00019B/3039